## I. Introduction

Gasoline "divorcement" statutes restrict -- and in their most extreme form, proscribe -- the vertical integration of gasoline refiners and gasoline retailers. Divorcement laws are currently in effect in six states (Hawaii, Connecticut, Delaware, Maryland, Nevada, Virginia), and the District of Columbia, and have been considered in many more. Since 1974, divorcement bills have come before forty-one state legislatures; currently, both San Francisco and San Diego are considering whether to impose such restrictions.

Historically, divorcement legislation has been rationalized as a means for preventing "predation" on the part of refiner-owned service stations against their franchised dealers. This theory is difficult to reconcile with economic analysis. Predation normally is thought of as an action taken against a *rival* for the purpose of eliminating that rival as a competitive constraint, thereby conferring (additional) market power upon the predator. Thus, it is possible to imagine one refiner engaging in predation against another refiner, or a retailer preying upon a rival retailer. But it would make little sense for a refiner to prey upon its affiliated retailers. These retailers are not the refiner's competitive constraint; other refiners are. Even a refiner possessing substantial market power has no incentive to drive its efficient dealers out of business -- to the contrary, refiner profits will be maximized only when wholesale and retail distribution is efficient.[1]

------------

[1] A given refiner might wish to eliminate the retailers of *rival* refiners, but this would be a means to the end result of eliminating the rival refiner. Moreover,

(continued...)

Although the notion of predatory behavior by refiners against retailers makes little sense, it is possible nonetheless to construct a public policy rationale for divorcement policies that is potentially reconcilable with a well-specified model of economic behavior.[2] Recent theoretical models have established the possibility of welfare-reducing vertical integration.[3] If behavior in wholesale and retail gasoline markets is well-described by such models, then it is possible that divorcement policies could result in greater equilibrium output than would occur absent the restrictions on vertical integration.

The alternative explanation for joint ownership of refiners and retailers is that integration creates economic efficiency. The economics literature has identified numerous efficiency-enhancing motives for vertical integration, such as eliminating

_____

[1] (...continued)
proponents of divorcement do not appear concerned by this interbrand effect -- rather, they appear to be motivated by the elimination of "intrabrand" competition (*e.g.*, a refiner-owned Mobil station eliminating an independent Mobil dealer).

[2] Somewhat more plausibly, one could perhaps view divorcement statutes as a means for protecting retailers against "hold-ups" by their affiliated refiners. This theory is only marginally more satisfactory than the "predation" theory, however. Generally speaking, when relationship-specific investments create the risk of opportunism, it is in the mutual interest of both parties to create contractual arrangements to mitigate this risk (*see, e.g.,* Klein, Crawford, and Alchian (1978)). Failure to do so raises the total cost of producing and distributing the product, thus reducing the manufacturer's total profits.

[3] *See, e.g.,* Salinger (1988). For a critical review of this literature, see Reiffen and Vita (1995).

double marginalization;[4] reducing transactions costs;[5] preventing opportunism;[6] and eliminating input distortions.[7] If the integration of refiners and retailers represents an attempt to attain these efficiencies, policies that proscribe or limit this integration will result in costs and prices higher than would otherwise obtain.

This paper attempts to differentiate empirically between these competing theories. I estimate a reduced form equation for the real retail price of unleaded regular

---

[4] *See* Spengler (1950). More recently, models have been constructed in which producers deliberately endow their retailers with market power (*e.g.,* through the granting of exclusive territories), and thereby induce double marginalization, yet nonetheless increase their profits by doing so (*see* Bonanno and Vickers (1988); Rey and Stiglitz (1995)). The logic is as follows: by granting their retailers (downstream) market power, each producer reduces its demand elasticity, leading to higher equilibrium upstream prices.

If the market for gasoline refining and retailing were conducive to these arrangements, divorcement statutes seemingly would be unnecessary, for refiners would then have a private incentive to avoid integration into retailing. It might be argued, however, that producers could find themselves in a prisoners' dilemma, whereby joint profits would be maximized if all refiners eschewed vertical integration, but where noncooperative behavior results in an equilibrium with a (privately) excessive degree of vertical integration. In this case, divorcement regulations might enforce the joint-profit maximizing "no integration" equilibrium.

This scenario is implausible, however, for two reasons. First, as a theoretical matter, this prisoners' dilemma does not arise in either the Bonanno and Vickers model or the Rey and Stiglitz model – in both models, producers have a unilateral, as well as a joint, incentive to avoid vertical integration. Second, there is little evidence that integrated gasoline refiners favor divorcement policies, as they likely would if the primary effect of divorcement laws was to attenuate this prisoners' dilemma. Rather, most of the political pressure for divorcement appears to come from independent retailers.

[5] Coase (1937).

[6] *See*, for example, Monteverde and Teece, (1982a) and (1982b); and Klein (1988).

[7] Examples include Mallela and Nahata (1980) and Westfield (1981).

gasoline using state-level monthly data covering the period 1995-97. Controlling for other exogenous determinants of retail price, I find that divorcement regulations raise the price of gasoline by about 2.7¢ per gallon, resulting in a sacrifice of consumers' surplus of over $100 million annually. This finding is consistent with the earlier empirical literature on the effects of retail divorcement, and strongly suggests that current proposals to divorce gasoline retailing from refining will be detrimental to consumers' interests.[8]

## II. Background and Literature Review

As a general matter, proscribing integration between upstream and downstream firms will affect prices, outputs, and profits if (1) linear pricing of the input fails to maximize the sum of buyer and seller profits; and (2) contractual alternatives to vertical integration (such as two-part tariffs) do not perfectly substitute for vertical integration as a means for maximizing this joint profit.[9] The literature on contractual arrangements between refiners and retailers of gasoline has identified several reasons why a principal-agent problem may arise in the relationship between these parties, and why contractual solutions to this problem may be imperfect.

---

[8] *See* Goldstein, Gold, and Kleit (1998) for a discussion of recent divorcement proposals.

[9] See generally Tirole (1988), ch. 4.

In choosing a vertical structure, the general problem facing the refiner is that retail output is a function of downstream sales efforts by the station manager and of downstream prices. Because these determinants of downstream demand differ in the extent to which they can be observed and contractually-specified, the contractual form chosen to govern the relationship between a refiner and a particular retailer will be determined to a significant extent by the product and service mix offered by the retailer. Barron and Umbeck (1984, 1985) and, to a greater extent, Shepard (1990, 1993) discuss why principal-agent problems may be present in the refiner-retailer relationship, and why heterogeneity across retailer types (*e.g.*, full service vs. self-service) yields, in equilibrium, diversity in the contractual form governing the refiner-retailer relationship.

Shepard (1993, p. 60) argues that, in general, independent retailers seldom would choose the effort levels or (because of double-marginalization problems) prices that are optimal from the perspective of the refiner. To ameliorate its retailers' moral hazard, the refiner must choose a contract that either specifies directly the desired outcome (*e.g.*, the retail price) or achieves incentive compatibility through indirect methods. Some elements of retailer performance will not be amenable to low-cost contractual solutions (*e.g.*, sales efforts); others (*e.g.*, retail price) will be more so, although even here there will be legal and economic constraints on the ability to obtain contractually the first-best outcome.[10] Shepard argues that where unobservable (hence noncontractable) demand-increasing efforts by on-site managers are an important element of retail demand, contractual arrangements that make this manager the residual claimant to the attendant profits -- either "lessee-dealer" or "open-dealer" contracts -- will be preferred.[11] This situation is likely to arise where, for example, the station provides full repair services in addition to gasoline sales.

By contrast, where unobservable retailer efforts are less important -- for example, at self-service, gasoline-only stations -- the principal rationale for vertical restraints would be elimination of double-marginalization problems (Shepard, 1993, p. 63). In principle, this could be addressed through contract, since retail price is observable; however, as noted above, until recently there have been legal limits on maximum RPM contracts. Although there are alternative contractual mechanisms available (*e.g.*, minimum quantities, two-part tariffs), they are imperfect substitutes.[12] Elimination of

---

[10] For example, until recently maximum resale price maintenance contracts were illegal *per se*. *See State Oil Co. v. Khan*, 522 U.S. 3 (1997). Two-part prices are legal, but may not be first-best if contractors are not risk-neutral (Barron and Umbeck, 1984, p. 318). Moreover, as Shepard notes (1993), attainment of the first-best may require a different contract for each retailer. This may be prohibitively costly.

[11] With "lessee-dealer" contracts, land and immobile capital assets are owned by the refiner, who leases the property to the retailer. The refiner typically sets the wholesale gasoline price, the property rental rate, and minimum monthly wholesale gasoline volumes. With "open-dealer" contracts, the retailer owns the physical assets. The refiner establishes the wholesale price and minimum volumes. *See* Shepard (1993, p. 62).

[12] *See* Tirole (1988, p. 176).

the double markup may be most easily resolved by means of refiner ownership of the retail outlet.

In terms of its predictions for retail price, this analysis suggests that prices will be lower at company-owned outlets, *ceteris paribus*, and therefore that proscribing company ownership will result in an increase in prices not only at those stations that would have been company-owned, but also at rivals of those stations. The empirical analyses contained in Barron and Umbeck (1984, 1985) and Shepard (1993) are consistent with this prediction. Barron and Umbeck compared pre- and post-divorcement pricing behavior of gasoline stations in Maryland. They found that at stations that had been company-owned before the enactment of the legislation, full-service prices rose 6.7¢ (relative to competitors); self-service prices rose 1.4¢ (1984, p. 323). They also found that prices at competing stations also rose post-divorcement. Similarly, Shepard (1993, pp. 69-71) found that company-owned stations charged lower prices than their nonintegrated counterparts; this differential ranged from 1.35¢ to almost 10¢ per gallon.

Although Shepard and Barron and Umbeck found vertical integration associated with lower retail prices, models have been constructed in which partial vertical integration is anticompetitive, and therefore where divorcement policies potentially could induce lower equilibrium prices.[13] These models typically posit imperfect competition (*i.e.*, positive price-cost margins) at both the upstream and downstream

---

[13] *See, e.g.*, Salinger (1988); Ordover *et al.* (1990); Hart and Tirole (1991).

stages of production in the pre-integration competitive environment. A merger of an upstream and downstream firm is undertaken, which causes the integrated entity's costs to fall (because the input is now transferred at marginal cost). If the upstream affiliate of the vertically integrated entity can commit to no longer selling to other downstream firms (*e.g.,* as in Salinger (1988)), the nonintegrated upstream firms may have the ability to increase prices to these buyers. Offsetting this, however, is the fact that the derived demand curve facing these sellers will shift leftward, owing to the expansion of output by the integrated entity. In equilibrium, retail prices may rise or fall; so might input prices. One possible outcome is for the input prices facing unintegrated firms to rise at the same time downstream prices fall (*see, e.g.,* Reiffen and Vita (1995)). Though consumers would benefit from vertical integration in this particular outcome, this equilibrium would be consistent with complaints from unintegrated dealers that they frequently find themselves caught in a price-cost "squeeze."

From a theoretical perspective, then, divorcement laws could have either a positive or negative effect on retail prices. If the principal effect of the law is to attenuate anticompetitive vertical "foreclosure," one should expect to observe lower equilibrium prices in divorcement states than in nondivorcement states *ceteris paribus*. The opposite result should obtain if the divorcement policies prevent refiners and retailers from realizing efficiencies that can be obtained only through vertical integration. In what follows, I attempt to discriminate between these competing

hypotheses by specifying and estimating an empirical model of retail gasoline prices.

### III. The Empirical Model

I attempt to analyze the competitive effects of divorcement legislation by

estimating a reduced form price equation with time series-cross section data on state

average gasoline prices. I estimate an equation of the following general form:

$$P_{it} \cdot f(demand\ shifters_{it},\ cost\ shifters_{it},\ regulation\ dummies_{it}) \qquad [1]$$

where $P_{it}$ is the (average) retail price of gas, net of taxes, in state $i$ and period $t$; demand

and cost shifters (discussed in greater detail below) represent exogenous determinants

of gasoline demand and supply; and "regulation dummies" are variables indicating the

presence or absence of certain types of regulations affecting petroleum retailing. In this

specification, the equilibrium impact of the divorcement statute would be captured by

the coefficient on the divorcement dummy variable. If the net effect of the legislation is

to eliminate efficiencies from vertical integration, then the coefficient on this dummy

variable will reflect the resulting upward shift in the retail cost function (i.e., the

coefficient will have a positive value). If the effect of the legislation is to reduce

opportunities for anticompetitive behavior (i.e., if it reduces price-cost margins relative to an environment where there are no restrictions on vertical integration), the coefficient should take on a negative value.

The dependent variable in this model is average monthly retail price (net of taxes), in state $i$, for regular unleaded gasoline, measured in cents per gallon. These data are obtained from the Energy Information Administration's *Petroleum Marketing Annual*, and cover the period January 1995-December 1997. The right-hand-side variables consist of:

*Demand Shifters*:

      1. DENSITY = population/square miles in state

      2. INCOME = real per capita personal income ($)

      3. POP = total population

      4. VEHICLES/POP = total number of motor vehicles in state/population

      4. DRIVERS/POP = total number licensed drivers in state/population

      6. %OVER65 = percentage of population over age 65

      7. %DRIVERS20-44 = percentage of licensed drivers age 20-44

      8. M1-M11 = month dummy variables

      9. YR1-YR2 = year dummy variables

*Cost Shifters:*

1. WAGERATE = real hourly earnings for retail employees in state ($/hour)

2. TRANSPORT = real imputed transportation cost (see discussion below), (¢/gallon)

3. CRUDE = real spot price of West Texas Intermediate crude oil ($/bbl.)

4. REFORMGAS = percentage of gasoline sold satisfying reformulated gasoline (RFG) requirements

5. OXYGENGAS = percentage of gasoline sold satisfying winter oxygenated gasoline requirements

6. HEATINGDAYS – heating degree days in Census region[14]

7. CARBGAS = dummy variable (= 1 if state = California and month/year • May 1996) to reflect imposition of California Air Resources Board refining standard

8. WEST = dummy variable for states west of Rockies (California, Oregon, Washington, Idaho, Montana, Wyoming, Nevada, Arizona, New Mexico, Colorado, and Utah);

9. NE = dummy variable for Pennsylvania, New Jersey, NewYork, and the New England states)

10. AK , HI = dummy variables for Alaska and Hawaii

---

[14] To compute a heating or cooling degree day, add the high and low temperature for a given day. Divide the result by 2 to get the average temperature, and subtract 65. If negative, this result is termed "heating degree days;" if positive, "cooling degree days." Thus, if on a given day the high temperature equaled 50, and the low 30, that day had 25 heating degree days.

*Regulatory Variables:*

      1. DIVORCE           = 1 if state had divorcement regulation; 0 otherwise

      2. SELFSERV        = percentage of gasoline sold through self-service pumps

The means and standard deviations of these variables are presented in Table 1. All nominal monetary values are deflated by the Consumer Price Index.

The basic specification of equation [1] reflects general theoretical considerations; the specific choice of explanatory variables reflects the findings of previously published estimates of gasoline demand.[15] Economic theory implies that gasoline demand in an area will depend in significant part upon the characteristics of the population living in that area. These population characteristics include total population size (**POP**); average per capita real income (**INCOME**); age distribution (**%OVER65**); vehicle ownership (**VEHICLES/POP**); and driving licensure (**DRIVERS/POP**). It is expected that gasoline demand (hence price) should increase with income, vehicle ownership, and licensure, and decline with population age.

Previous researchers (*e.g.,* Lin *et al.*, 1985) also have found that gasoline demand is influenced significantly by the population density (**DENSITY**). The impact of increased density on price is ambiguous *a priori*. Travel demand, hence derived gasoline demand, should fall as the population is increasingly concentrated in smaller

---

[15] *See* Espey (1996, 1998) and Lin (1985).

areas; moreover, there tend to be more alternative transportation modes available (*e.g.,* buses) in densely populated areas. Additionally, increased population density likely reduces costs of transporting fuel from the wholesale "rack" to retailers (since increased population density likely will be associated with increased station density). *Ceteris paribus*, these effects should induce a negative relationship between density and price.[16] Conversely, increased population density also leads to traffic congestion, hence increased fuel consumption per mile traveled, and higher land rental values. Both of these factors should contribute to higher fuel prices.

Last, month dummies are included to control for the substantial seasonal component of gasoline demand (*see, e.g.,* Borenstein and Shepard, 1996, p. 440); year dummies are included to control for unobservable determinants of price that vary intertemporally, but not cross-sectionally.

Equation [1] also incorporates exogenous determinants of cost. Obviously, a major determinant of gasoline costs is the price of crude oil. Following Borenstein and Shepard (1996), I use the price of West Texas Intermediate crude as the relevant price (although similar results are obtained when other spot prices (*e.g.,* Brent crude) are used). It is well documented that retail prices respond to crude prices with a lag

---

[16] Dealers' costs also might be a function of population density. *Ceteris paribus*, increased density might result in increased volume at a smaller number of dealers, allowing the latter to exploit economies of scale in retailing.

(Borenstein *et al.*, 1997); accordingly, I include current and lagged values of the crude price as regressors.[17]

Production and transportation costs of gasoline also will be affected by the demand for jointly produced products, such as home heating oil, the demand for which is weather-determined.[18] Accordingly, like Scheffman and Spiller (1987) and Borenstein *et al.*(1997), I include the number of heating degree days (**HEATINGDAYS**) as an exogenous determinant of gasoline production costs.

Another potentially important determinant of cross-sectional variation in gasoline prices are environmental regulations that affect gasoline production costs. The Clean Air Act Amendments of 1990 contained two primary requirements for cleaner gasoline. The first of these is the reformulated gasoline (RFG) program, which requires cleaner-burning RFG to be sold in the nine (now ten) worst "ozone nonattainment"

---

[17] Ideally, one also would like to control for the cost of transporting crude oil from the field to the refinery. Because I lack direct measures of these costs, I instead control for crude transport price variation with four dummy variables: **NE** (equal to one for Pennsylvania, New Jersey, NewYork, and the New England states); **WEST** (equal to one for California, Oregon, Washington, Idaho, Montana, Wyoming, Nevada, Arizona, New Mexico, Colorado, and Utah); **HI** (equal to one for Hawaii), and **AK** (equal to one for Alaska).

[18] *A priori*, it is not clear what sign the coefficient on **HEATINGDAYS** should have. According to Scheffman and Spiller (1987, p. 136) and Borenstein *et al.* (1997, p. 316), gasoline is refined as a by-product of home heating oil. Heating oil and gasoline are complements in production (*i.e.*, increasing the output of heating oil also leads to an increase in gasoline production), but substitutes in transportation (*i.e.*, when heating oil is in high demand, a greater amount of transportation capacity is allocated to heating oil).

areas, beginning January 1, 1995.[19] In addition to the nine cities where RFG was mandated, a number of other cities adopted the RFG program voluntarily. Because RFG is more expensive to refine than ordinary gasoline, I include as an explanatory variable (**REFORMGAS**) the percentage of gasoline sold that satisfies the reformulated gasoline requirements.

The 1990 Clean Air Act Amendments also require the sale of oxygenated gasoline during the winter months (usually November through February) in those areas designated as carbon monoxide nonattainment areas. To control for the cost impact of this requirement, I include a variable (**OXYGENGAS**) equal to the percentage of gasoline sold that fulfills the oxygenated gasoline standards.

A third regulatory variable reflects the special reformulated gasoline program instituted in California in 1996. Like the Federal RFG program, the California Air Resources Board (CARB) standard is designed to reduce emissions of volatile organic compounds and nitrogen oxides, both of which contribute to the creation of ground-level ozone. The CARB-standard gasoline is refined to a different standard than the RFG gas produced for the other nonattainment areas, and the requisite production technology has been embodied in a relatively small number of refineries. At the time the CARB requirements were imposed, it was estimated that the standards would add

---

[19] The original areas are Baltimore, Chicago, Hartford, Houston, Los Angeles, Milwaukee, New York, Philadelphia, and San Diego. Later, Sacramento was added to this list.

5¢ to 15¢/gallon to the production cost of gasoline.[20] To control for the impact of this regulation on equilibrium prices, I include a dummy variable (**CARBGAS**) that takes on a value of 1 for May 1996 and all subsequent periods for all California observations. Because the production costs of CARB gasoline are thought to have fallen over time, I also interact **CARBGAS** with a year dummy (equal to 1 for 1997).

A final determinant of the cost of retail gasoline is the transportation cost of shipping the gasoline from the refinery to the dealer. Typically, bulk gasoline is shipped either by pipeline or water transportation from the refinery gate to the wholesale supply terminals, from which the gasoline is dispensed into tanker trucks for final delivery to the retail dealer. Ideally, we would like to incorporate a direct measure of these transportation costs into the empirical analysis. While interstate oil pipeline tariffs are filed with the Federal Energy Regulatory Commission, and are thus publicly available, there is no comparable source of public information for intrastate pipelines or for spot tanker/barge rates. As an alternative, I impute the cost of transporting gasoline from the refinery to the terminal (**TRANSPORT**) as the difference between a spot refinery price and the average terminal (or "rack") price for each state, as reported by the Energy Information Administration.[21]

---

[20] *See* the *CAL/EPA Factsheet* at www.calepa.ca.gov/publications/factsheets/1997/cleangas.htm.

[21] For western states, I use the Los Angeles spot price. For midwest and southeastern states, I use the Gulf Coast spot price. For states in the Northeast, I use the New York Harbor spot price.

## IV. Empirical Findings

The parameters of equation [1] are estimated with state-level monthly data for the period January 1995 - December 1997. Because of the likely existence of serial correlation of the disturbances within each state, I estimate equation [1] using a feasible generalized least squares (FGLS) procedure that assumes a common autocorrelation parameter across states.[22] That is, I assume equation [1] takes the following form:

$$y_{it} \cdot X_{it}\beta \cdot e_{it}, \quad e_{it} \cdot ?e_{i,t\cdot 1} \cdot ?_{it}, \quad ?_{it} \cdot (0, s^2 I)$$

Table 2 presents several sets of estimated FGLS parameters of the gasoline price equation. Column (a) presents a restricted version of equation [1], with only the most basic demand and cost shifters included as explanatory variables. Column (b) adds lagged crude prices to the equation; Column (c) adds other characteristics of the market (*e.g.*, per capita motor vehicle ownership). Column (d) presents OLS estimates of the fully specified version of the pricing equation.

---

[22] Other panel data estimation procedures, such as OLS with state-specific dummy variables (*i.e.*, a fixed-effects model) are precluded by the fact that there is no within-state variation in the regulatory variables for the sample period used here.

The coefficients on most of the exogenous variables have signs consistent with prior expectations.[23] Current and lagged crude prices (**CRUDE, CRUDE_1, CRUDE_2**) are positively related to retail prices, as are the imputed transportation costs (**TRANSPORT**) and two of the three reformulated gasoline programs (**OXYGENGAS** and **CARBGAS**).[24] Increased population density (**DENSITY**) is negatively related to price. Motor vehicle ownership **(VEHICLES/POP)**, income (**INCOME**), and proportion of drivers aged 20 to 44 (**%DRIVERS20-44**) are all positively related to retail price, although none are different from zero at conventional levels of statistical significance. Some of these controls (**DRIVERS/POP, %OVER65,** and **WAGERATE)** have coefficients with unexpected signs, but only in the case of **WAGERATE** is the coefficient statistically significant. The coefficient on heating degree days (**HEATINGDAYS**) is positive and statistically significant.

The parameter estimates presented in Table 2 provide a clear pattern of evidence suggesting that retail prices are 2¢ -3¢ per gallon higher in states with divorcement laws than in states without such restrictions; the 95 percent confidence interval on the estimated **DIVORCE** parameter in column (c), the fully specified version of model estimated with the FGLS procedure, is approximately 1.3¢ to 4¢ per gallon. The null

------

[23] Exceptions are **WAGERATE** and **%DRIVERS20-44**. In neither case can we reject the null hypothesis that the true parameter is equal to zero.

[24] Contrary to expectations, however, the coefficient on **YR3\*CARBGAS** is positive, suggesting that the cost of refining CARB standard gasoline rose, rather than fell, over the course of the sample period.

hypothesis that divorcement laws have no effect on retail prices can be rejected at the 1 percent significance level.

Divorcement statutes thus appear to have had the effect of increasing equilibrium retail prices. It is difficult to construct a procompetitive characterization of this result. One possibility is that there is some unobserved (by the econometrician) average quality difference between dealers in divorcement and nondivorcement states that consumers value at (approximately) 2.7¢ per gallon. While this possibility is, by definition, untestable (if we could observe all relevant aspects of quality we would include this information in the form of additional regressors), it would seem unlikely, given available empirical information on the characteristics of company-owned versus independently-owned stations. Existing research suggests the former are more likely to have characteristics valued by gasoline purchasers than the latter. For example, Shepard (1993) found that in her sample, company-owned stations tended to have greater sales capacity than independently-owned stations;[25] other things equal, greater capacity suggests less time spent in a queue waiting for an open pump. Shepard also reported that the independent open-dealer stations tended to have older physical plants than other stations;[26] this suggests, among other things, that the company-owned and

---

[25] Shepard (1993, p. 67) reports that the average open-dealer station had the capacity to serve 3.6 cars at a time, versus 5 or more cars at other station types. In her sample, approximately 75 percent of the open-dealers had only a single island, whereas only about 30 percent of the other stations were single island.

[26] Shepard (1993, p. 68) reports that less than half of the open-dealers had been

(continued...)

19

lessee-dealer stations may tend to have newer restrooms and other facilities valued by customers. In earlier research, Barron and Umbeck (1984, p. 324) found that stations directly affected by divorcement reduced their hours of operation substantially after they were converted from company-owned to dealer-owned facilities. Slade (1998, Table 7) presents similar evidence; she found (via estimation of probit analysis of the type of contract governing the refiner-retailer relationship) that hours of operation was positively related to the probability that a station's price was set by the refiner.

The parameter estimates in Table 2 also strongly indicate that, as one might expect, prices vary considerably depending on the quantity of gasoline sold through self-service pumps. In 1993, the last year for which data are available, almost 90 percent of gasoline is sold as "self-serve" in the states where self-service is legal.[27] This means that in those states where self-service is banned (New Jersey and Oregon), the price of unleaded regular gasoline is more than 3¢ per gallon higher, as shown in column (c), than where it is not banned.

Using quantity data from the Energy Information Administration, price data from the *Lundberg Survey*, and elasticity estimates from Espey (1998), we can approximate the increase in consumers' surplus that would arise from eliminating

_____

[26] (...continued)
remodeled in the 3-year period preceding the collection of her data; by contrast, more than two-thirds of the other stations had undertaken some remodeling during this period.

[27] Source: *National Petroleum News*, Mid-June 1994.

divorcment regulations. Espey (1998, p. 279) provides estimates of the long-run price elasticity of gasoline demand that range from 0 to -2.72 (median = -0.43). Using these estimates, and annual volume data from the *EIA* (1999), we can compute the quantity increases that would be induced by the predicted 2.7¢/gallon price reduction that would accompany a relaxation of the divorcement restrictions. With this information, it is straightforward to calculate the attendant increase in Marshallian consumer surplus, which ranges from $111.4 million (assuming completely inelastic demand) to $115.4 million (assuming an elasticity of -2.72, Espey's upper bound). For the median elasticity estimate ($? = -0.43$), the corresponding surplus increase is approximately $112.0 million. Calculated at the upper bound of the 95 percent confidence interval on **DIVORCE** (4.02¢/gallon), the increase in surplus (evaluated at $? = -0.43$) rises to over $112 million annually.

It should be noted that these estimates are a lower bound on the welfare increase that would result from deregulation of the refiner-retailer relationship. These calculations correspond to the consumption of unleaded regular gasoline. Though we have not estimated the effects of divorcement deregulation for the price and quantity of mid-grade and premium fuel, it is quite likely that deregulation would engender decreases in the prices of these products as well. Given that these higher-grade fuels account for almost one-third of total gasoline sales, the consumer surplus associated with these price changes would be substantial.

## V. Conclusion

Although divorcement regulation has been imposed in only six states, there is recurrent interest in this policy, particularly in areas (*e.g.*, San Francisco, San Diego) where retail prices appear "inexplicably" high (Goldstein, Gold, and Kleit, 1998; Borenstein and Gilbert, 1993). As noted in the introduction, while it is possible theoretically for vertical integration to result in noncompetitive equilibria, previous empirical studies of divorcement not only fail to show that such policies result in lower prices, they indicate strongly that divorcement results in prices significantly higher than would have obtained had no such restrictions been imposed. This suggests that the integration of refiners and retailers is a source of economic efficiency that is foregone when integration is restricted or proscribed.

The analysis presented here reaffirms these earlier findings. Using state-level data for the middle-1990s, I find that divorcement regulations increased the retail price of unleaded regular gasoline by more than 2.7¢ per gallon. While this number might seem small, it must be borne in mind, as Borenstein and Gilbert (1993) emphasize, that a relatively small distortion can translate into a rather sizable aggregate welfare loss in a large market. Annual retail sales of gasoline exceed $147 billion per year. Were divorcement policies imposed via national legislation (as has been proposed in recent years), the annual consumer welfare loss could come to approximately $2.5 billion per year. This is a large price to pay for a policy having no evident benefits.

# References

Barron, John and John Umbeck, "The Effects of Different Contractual Arrangements: The Case of Retail Gasoline Markets," *Journal of Law & Economics* 27 (1984), 313-28.

Barron, John, Mark Loewenstein, and John Umbeck, "Predatory Pricing: The Case of the Retail Gasoline Market," *Contemporary Policy Issues* 3 (1985), 130-39.

Bonanno, Giacomo, and John Vickers, "Vertical Separation," *Journal of Industrial Economics* 36 (1988), 257-65.

Borenstein, Severin, and Richard Gilbert, "Uncle Sam at the Gas Pump: Causes and Consequences of Regulating Gasoline Distribution," *Regulation* (1993), 63-75.

Borenstein, Severin, A. Colin Cameron, and Richard Gilbert, " Do Gasoline Prices Respond Asymetrically to Crude Oil Price Changes?," *Quarterly Journal of Economics* 112 (1997), 305-39.

Borenstein, Severin and Andrea Shepard, "Dynamic Pricing in Retail Gasoline Markets," *RAND Journal of Economics* 27 (1996), 429-51.

Coase, Ronald, "The Theory of the Firm," *Economica* n.s. 4 (1937), 386-405.

Energy Information Administration, *Petroleum Marketing Annual*, 1999.

Espey, Molly, "Explaining the Variation in Elasticity Estimates of Gasoline Demand in the United States: A Meta-Analysis," *Energy Journal* 17 (1996), 49-60.

_____. "Gasoline Demand Revisited: An International Meta-Analysis of Elasticities," *Energy Economics* 20 (1998), 273-95.

Goldstein, Larry, Ron Gold, and Andrew Kleit, "Divorced From the Facts: Retail Gasoline Divorcement Redux," *Oil & Gas Journal*, November 9, 1998, 27-34.

Hart, Oliver, and Jean Tirole, "Vertical Integration and Market Foreclosure," *Brookings Papers on Economic Activity*, 1990, 205-86.

Honeycutt, T. Crawford, "Competition in Controlled and Uncontrolled Gasoline Markets," *Contemporary Policy Issues* 3 (1985), 105-39.

Klein, Benjamin, Robert Crawford, and Armen Alchian, "Vertical Integration, Appropriable Rents, and the Competitive Contracting Process," *Journal of Law & Economics* 21 (1978), 297-326.

Klein, Benjamin, "Vertical Integration as Organizational Ownership: The Fisher Body-General Motors Relationship Revisited," *Journal of Law, Economics, & Organization* (1988), 199-213.

Lin, An Loh *et al.*, "State Gasoline Consumption in the USA: An Econometric Analysis," *Energy Economics* 7 (1985), 29-36.

Mallela, Parthasaradhi and Babu Nahata, "Theory of Vertical Control With Variable Proportions," *Journal of Political Economy* 88 (1980), 1009-25.

Monteverde, Kirk, and David J. Teece, "Supplier Switching Costs and Vertical Integration in the Automobile Industry," 13 *Bell Journal of Economics* (1982), 206-13.

_____, "Appropriable Rents and Quasi-Vertical Integration," 25 *Journal of Law & Economics* 25 (1982) 321-28.

Ordover, Janusz *et al.*, "Equilibrium Vertical Foreclosure," *American Economic Review* 80 (1990), 127-42.

Reiffen, David and Michael Vita, "Is There New Thinking on Vertical Mergers?," *Antitrust Law Journal* 63 (1995), 917-41.

Rey, Patrick and Joseph Stiglitz, "The Role of Exclusive Territories in Producers' Competition," *RAND Journal of Economics* 26 (1995), 431-51.

Salinger, Michael, "Vertical Mergers and Market Foreclosure," *Quarterly Journal of Economics* 103 (1988), 345-56.

Shepard, Andrea "Pricing Behavior and Vertical Contracts in Retail Markets," *American Economic Review (Papers and Proceedings),* 80 (1990), 427-31.

_____, "Contractual Form, Retail Price, and Asset Characteristics," *RAND Journal of Economics* 24 (1993), 58-77.

Slade, Margaret, "Strategic Motives for Vertical Separation," *Journal of Law, Economics, & Organization* 14 (1998), 84-113.

Spengler, Joseph, "Vertical Integration and Antitrust Policy," *Journal of Political Economy* 58 (1950), 347-52.

Tirole, Jean, *The Theory of Industrial Organization*, (Cambridge: MIT Press),1988.

Westfield, J. Fred, "Vertical Integration: Does Product Price Rise or Fall?," *American Economic Review* 71 (1981), 334-46.

## Table 1

## Descriptive Statistics

| Variable Name | Mean | Standard Deviation |
|---|---|---|
| R_RETAIL | 51.43 | 6.23 |
| DENSITY | 172.62 | 235.68 |
| VEHICLES/POP | 0.82 | 0.12 |
| DRIVERS/POP | 0.69 | 0.05 |
| %DRIVERS20-44 | 0.52 | 0.03 |
| %OVER65 | 0.12 | 0.02 |
| INCOME | 14907.2 | 2255.2 |
| WAGERATE | 7.99 | .89 |
| TRANSPORT | 4.42 | 2.89 |
| CRUDE | 12.83 | 1.24 |
| HEATINGDAYS | 4900.16 | 1783.16 |
| REFORMGAS | .18 | .33 |
| OXYGENGAS | 0.03 | .11 |

# Table 2

Retail Price Regression

Monthly Data, 1995-97

Dependent Variable = Real Price Unleaded Regular Gasoline, Net of Taxes, in ¢/gallon

| Variable | Coefficient (t-statistic) (a) | Coefficient (t-statistic) (b) | Coefficient (t-statistic) (c) | Coefficient (t-statistic) (d) |
|---|---|---|---|---|
| DIVORCE | 2.11 (3.59) | 1.91 (3.59) | 2.67 (3.89) | 2.08 (6.28) |
| SELFSERV | -2.07 (-2.57) | -2.07 (-2.57) | -3.43 (-3.71) | -2.92 (-6.96) |
| DENSITY | | | -0.003 (-3.09) | -0.004 (-7.84) |
| POP | | | -5.66 (-1.49) | -3.69 (-2.01) |
| VEHICLES/POP | | | 0.73 (0.52) | 1.31 (1.92) |
| DRIVERS/POP | | | -3.87 (-1.12) | -4.17 (-2.37) |
| %DRIVERS20-44 | | | 2.00 (0.21) | -0.65 (-0.14) |
| %OVER65 | | | 0.23 (1.59) | 0.24 (3.52) |
| INCOME | -0.00008 (-0.92) | -0.00004 (-0.46) | 0.0001 (0.84) | 0.0001 (1.79) |
| WAGERATE | -0.092 (-0.65) | -0.13 (-0.90) | -0.29 (-2.00) | -0.25 (−3.10) |
| TRANSPORT | 0.27 (12.36) | 0.23 (12.26) | 0.21 (11.53) | 0.35 (12.21) |
| CRUDE | 1.02 (16.87) | 0.79 (13.77) | 0.78 (20.75) | 0.62 (5.83) |
| CRUDE(-1) | | 1.21 (20.06) | 1.22 (20.75) | 1.02 (8.12) |
| CRUDE(-2) | | 0.59 (11.29) | 0.59 (11.51) | 0.65 (7.10) |
| HEATINGDAYS | | | 0.0005 (4.29) | 0.0004 (7.60) |

| Variable | Coefficient (t-statistic) (a) | Coefficient (t-statistic) (b) | Coefficient (t-statistic) (c) | Coefficient (t-statistic) (d) |
|---|---|---|---|---|
| REFORMGAS | -0.41 (-1.37) | -0.45 (-1.74) | -0.19 (-0.72) | 1.06 (3.32) |
| OXYGENGAS | 1.29 (2.06) | 0.75 (1.27) | 0.56 (0.96) | 3.02 (4.60) |
| CARBGAS | 1.21 (0.98) | 0.54 (0.48) | 1.95 (1.67) | 0.34 (0.35) |
| CARBGAS*YR3 | 0.37 (0.26) | 1.32 (1.06) | 1.92 (1.54) | 0.60 (0.55) |
| AK | 24.66 (27.82) | 24.48 (25.76) | 26.26 (20.52) | 25.07 (41.09) |
| HI | 15.38 (15.85) | 15.97 (15.45) | 15.85 (13.71) | 14.91 (24.05) |
| WEST | 5.79 (18.09) | 5.80 (17.13) | 5.89 (15.29) | 5.60 (30.14) |
| NE | 2.55 (5.83) | 2.39 (5.11) | 1.75 (3.27) | 1.70 (6.91) |
| CONSTANT | 37.36 (21.23) | 16.44 (8.12) | 13.29 (2.24) | 16.94 (5.61) |
| autocorrelation coefficient | 0.6865 | 0.7571 | 0.7684 | na |
| $R^2$ | na | na | na | 0.85 |
| Log Likelihood | -3474.48 | -2976.13 | -2934.36 | na |

Coefficients in columns (a)-(c) estimated with feasible generalized least squares assuming homoskedasticity and a constant autocorrelation coefficient across states. Coefficients in column (d) estimated with ordinary least squares. Coefficients on month and year dummies not shown.